Living up to your Christian Potential

Motivational Poems & Quotes to Strengthen Your Walk with Christ

By Jill E. Porter

I dedicate this book to my Savior.

A special thanks to my daughter - Jennifer S. Hossman
My Granddaughter - Kristen M. Hubbell
My Grandson - Kyle T. Kelley
Pastor Pat Wallace
and
Pastor Bill Hossman
For all of their spiritual support and love.
No part of this book can be reproduced.

Written and illustrated by
Jill E. Porter
Jennifer S. Porter

© 2016

Foreword:

Everyone is faced with doubt and fear on a daily basis. As a Christian, these things can hinder our relationship with God. We strive to be a beacon of his light for the world, but our struggles can sometimes weaken our light or even stamp it out completely. Sometimes we just need a word of motivation or encouragement from a fellow believer. As I sit in daily prayer and communion, so many words of motivation come to mind. I believe if I can get these words to as many children of God as possibly, if I can encourage even one person to continue to walk in faith and fight the good fight, then I am letting my beacon shine bright. If you are tired today, dragged down by the situation of our society, swimming in doubt from every direction; then, take a minute or even five and lose yourself in spiritual motivation. It only takes one kind word to change someone's whole day. I hope to do that for you.

In His light

Motivational Poems and Expressions

Walking Through Another Valley

We must learn the word of God and use it at all times. Apply it where it is needed and get it deep into the roots of our heart and soul. Always remember, the word of God is the sword of truth for the days of our battles and it is very powerful. We need to learn how to use everything that God gives us including wisdom and knowledge. We need to understand the spirit of the Lord, the spirit of His counsel, and the spirit of courage. We must maintain balance when a problem arises. Don't allow any person or situation to get into your spirit or it will get a hold and take control of your emotions and heart. Your life is going to be full of surprises and tough situations. We must learn to endure them. Endure means to remain firm under suffering without yielding. Walking through another valley is a true test of our faith. As we are walking through, we will discover that our faith is our life support. It is also a test of our spiritual and emotional well being. Each new valley is a life situation designed to teach us, strengthen our character, and renew our spiritual virtues. It helps us stretch our wings and grow into greater potential. God is a watcher and an observer of humanity. He knows and sees all.

Is All to Me

O blessed Christ, my strength, my King
He is my comfort and my stay
In Him I hope, of Him I sing
While toiling over life's rugged ways
He is the God almighty, and great He is
For Christ, my King, is all to me

You Have to Believe

Physical, financial, and emotional challenges are a real part of our everyday lives. They can create boundaries that inhibit our spiritual growth. God has given us His word to move beyond these boundaries in faith. Your life is a reflection of what you believe. If you believe that someone or something can stop you, then it can and it will. What you believe is a foundation of what you can do. There is nothing so wrong that it cannot be righted and lifted from your spirit. There is nothing so bad, horrible, and ugly that you can't work through, but you must believe. Believing in the Lord is above the range of known possibility and probability.

The Tornado

The birds had stopped singing; the earth was still.
The sky was so dark that it gave me a chill.
On the radio was a tornado warning;
I'd been listening since early morning.
Oh, what should I do and where should I go?
I'm so forgetful that I'll never know.
I secured the windows, then locked the door.
I said a prayer and then fell to the floor.
With faith in my Lord, I weathered the storm.
He kept me close by, dry and warm.
The tornado has made my faith grow stronger; and through God I can live a little longer.
For many there was death and destruction.
They say there will be a lot of new construction.
But God in His mercy heard my plea.
How fortunate I am. Don't you agree?

The Hands

The hands that created the world and gave us the sun, the moon, and the light
Are the tiny hands of a baby born on a cold December night?
The hands that held the powers to break the binding chains of sin
Are the gentle hands that washed the feet of the tired and dusty men.
The hands that shaped the universe and created the stars in space
Are the hands of a dying man who suffered and took our place?
The hands of our creator, Lord, and King of Kings above
Are the hands that are forever reaching out to us with His love.

Spilling the Milk

When you spill the milk, God will give you the means to clean it up. The means is the truth, faith, discipline, and obedience of His words to you. Sometimes we are courageous enough to face the messes that we create in our own lives and clean them up. Sometimes we try to ignore the mess and turn a blind eye to the truth. When we ignore our messes, God doesn't get angry. He gives us the means again and encourages us to tell the truth and admit our faults. If you make the mess again and again, God will continue to give you the means to right your wrongs and wait patiently for you to do so. Too often we count on God to clean up our messes for us. We may even whine, plead, or cry but God simply waits on us because He knows when we get tired of living in our mess, we will clean it up and stop spilling the milk.

The Choice is Ours
Think about all that God is. God is love, peace, joy, strength, power, abundance, and truth. God is not pain, anger, or confusion. So often we find ourselves in painful, frightening, or destructive situations that can limit our freedom or make us unhappy. For some reason we convince ourselves that we are where God wants us to be. Remember, if it is not love, peace, joy, and harmony; it is not of God. When we make a choice to stay in a harmful, abusive, or painful environment, it is not where God wants us to be. God cannot help us until we are ready to accept His help. He wants only the best for us because he loves us. The choice is ours.

Pretend and Play
I made a house in the woods and no one could ever find it. I would stay there for countless hours and quietly I would play. I loved going to the meadow and picking morning glories, daffodils, daisies, and tiger lilies. Then, I would take toothpicks and make pretty dolls of Many Colors. While I was making dolls, I could hear a robin singing deep in a small Valley within a ravine far away. His song sounded like a soft and beautiful Symphony Orchestra. Before I knew it, the sun will begin to disappear and the night would unfold around me. I would make plans for another day so I could pretend and play.

For Mila Elaine Kelley,
Love in Jesus,
Nana 6/15/18

My Nana
I like to walk with Nana because her steps are short like mine. She doesn't say now hurry lad. She always takes her time. Most people have to hurry. They don't take time to see, all of God's beauty that He has for you and me. So, the next time you see us, stop and say hello, for we are true friends forever because my Nana tells me so.
TO MY GREAT GRANDSON
VANN RYAN HUBBELL
LOVE IN JESUS ALWAYS, NANA

Truth is My First Line of Defense
In thee let joy with beauty and strength united with love The eagles' wings folding around the warm heart of a dove. The sky is as a temple's arch in the blue and wavy air It is glorious with the Spirit march of messengers of prayer God is in my every tomorrow therefore, I live for today Certain at finding as sunrise is guidance and strength for my way. Power for each moment of weakness, hope for each moment of pain. Comfort for every sorrow, sunshine and joy after the rain

Break Through
Break thru darkness with light. Jesus is the light of the world.
Break thru morning with joy. Your sorrow will turn into joy.
Break thru despair with comfort. The Father of mercies is the God of all comfort.
Break thru hurt with hope. This hope we have is our anchor.
Break thru a heart that has been broken. He has sent me to heal the brokenhearted.

What I Would Really Miss

Oh, dear Lord, it seems like it was just yesterday that my children played upon the floor, and I would wipe countless fingerprints from the window panes and doors. I kissed away a thousand tears and tried to keep pace with my hands. Then I would race around the clock until the day would come to an end. I would sit in my rocking chair and rock for countless hours. I would think how nice it would be when my children were all grown and the time would be my own. Now, I sit and I rock alone with all my work done. No little tots on the floor, no fingerprints on the window panes or doors, no boo-boos or bruises to kiss. Oh my, how could I know what I would really miss?

A Mother's Love

A mother's love is something that no one can explain.
It is made up of deep devotion, sacrifice, and pain.
It is endless, selfless, and enduring come what may.
Nothing can destroy it or take that love away.
It is patient and forgiving when all others are forsaking.
It never fails or falters even through a heart that's breaking.
It believes beyond when the world around condemns.
It grows with all the beauty of life's rarest gems.

He Always Will

It's amazing and incredible, but it's true as it can be.
God loves and understands us all, that means you and me.
His grace is all-sufficient for both the young and old.
For the lonely and the timid, for the brash and the bold.
His love knows no exceptions, so never feel excluded.
No matter who or what you are, your name has been included.

And no matter what your past has been, trust God to understand.
And no matter what your problem is, just place it in His hand.
For in all of our unloveliness, this great God loves us still.
He loved us since the beginning of this world and what's more; He always will.

I Never Dust My Bible Anymore
On cleaning day, I would dust my Bible then put it back on the shelf for all to see. I wanted it to have that much-used look, but reading it just wasn't for me. The Holy Spirit came to me and said, study your book and then spread the Good News. For you know that Bible has not been read; this Book was surely meant for you to use. I opened the Book and found treasure that I had surely never dreamed was there. Within its pages was without measure the truth that I had been seeking elsewhere. Now my Bible is getting worn and I am much happier than before. However, when it came to cleaning morn, I never dust my Bible anymore.

An Open Gate
There's an open gate at the end of the road.
Through it, each one must go alone.
And there in the light we cannot see,
Our Father claims His own.
Beyond the gate you'll always be loved.
And find happiness and rest.
And there is comfort in the thought,
That our loving God knows best.

The Stars

I can remember the warm summer nights outside as I would sit on the front porch in the presence of the Lord. The wind was silent and I could hear the sound of the crickets and peace would come over my heart and soul. It was a time of intimacy alone with the Lord and it was so inspiring to me. As the sun would disappear and the moon would rise, the night unfolds and the stars appear in the sky. As I looked up towards heaven, I could see God's creation; the stars. Each star looked like a beacon of hope; it was an enchanting and timeless beauty that God created. What I saw that night was a blessed gift; it reminded me that God created it all.

Faith of my Child

My little girl fell and hurt her knee.
Then suddenly she came running to me.
Mommy, will God make the scrape go away?
Oh, mommy, will you please help me pray?
Confused, I didn't know what to say.
I hadn't prayed for many a day.
Well now, mothers of course always know
What is best for their children, and so
I washed her knee and mumbled a prayer.
I said the words and her faith was there.
Well her knee got well, but to this day,
I think her faith taught me how to pray.
TO JENNIFER HOSSMAN
MY BELOVED DAUGHTER
LOVE, MOMMY

Ten Little Fingers and Ten Little Toes
Ten little fingers and ten little toes, Two wee ears and a tiny little nose.
Two beautiful eyes of midnight blue, and there on your face was a dimple or two.
This miracle so hard to explain, God blessed me over and over again.
He made me a mother and a grandmother it's true, this most unworthy one is grateful to You.
Thank you, God, for my loving child and my grandchildren: Jennifer, Kristen, and Kyle

Beautiful Memories of the Past
A little girl was walking down a long and dusty lane.
Her mother stood by the back door to welcome her home again.
She had an apron tied around her waist and silver in her hair.
And coming from the kitchen was a fragrance of freshly baked bread that filled the air.
Her father was dressed in his blue overalls that he loved to wear.
And deep within his heart, he always had love to share.
Her sister played with dolls and make-up and dressed in fancy clothes.
She loved music and her little sister because that is the life she chose.
Her brother enjoyed working on cars and loved playing sports of all kinds.
Sometimes our mother would make him babysit us when he had other things in mind.
As I sit and start thinking about the beautiful memories of the past,
I knew deep within my heart that they would always last.

Thank you, God for blessing me with a beloved family. Charlie, Catherine, Jerry and Jane Porter. Love in Jesus, Jill

Hummingbirds

They are nature's little helicopter and they are really a sight to see. As they put their bodies into action, flying high and low to the ground and the trees. Doing figure eights with the tips of their wings, making a buzzing and a humming sound and doing about anything. They have to eat as much as their weight from the nectar of the flowers, so they can keep up their high-octane fuel that gives them a lot of power. Their singing, well, is quite a song to hear through and through. They can chirp, whistle, bob-o-leak, squeak, and zing like a riffle too. They can sing in a group or sing by themselves while they are enjoying the wonderful view. Aren't you glad that God gave us one of life's simplest pleasures. He created the hummingbird for all our hearts to treasure.

The Teacher on the Cross

You were humiliated before the throne, please teach me to be humble.
You bore great punishment but did no wrong, please help me not to stumble.
Even to death your boundless love was there, please teach me charity.
You have proven that God is everywhere, please keep giving me faith to see.
And still your forgiveness has no boundary, please keep teaching me to forgive.
Oh, what wondrous way you died for me, please keep teaching me how to live.

Fond Memories
Years have passed since I left my homestead, But there are a few fond memories that will linger on. The narrow roads that I walked without fear, As my daddy and I held hands we were so close and near. We would see all kinds of flowers in bloom at the top of the hill, even wild blueberry patches and wild daffodils. Lots of mountains and sparkling cool streams, tall graceful pine trees in nature's beauty serene. Then winter would come and the snowflakes would fall on the ground, they would be all different sizes and shapes, but they would never make a sound. I thank God for all the fond memories, they will never fade away, For they have been planted deep within my heart and soul and they are always here to stay.

Motivational Quotes and Prayers

- The suffering servant became steeped in loneliness and pain, but he bore for me in grief and shame a crown of thorns and a heavy cross.
- Jesus loves us with purity, consistency, and passion no matter how imperfect we are.
- When we say that we remain in Jesus Christ, it means that we believe He is the son of God.
- I'll go in the strength of the Lord in paths he has marked for my feet. I'll follow the light of His word and not shrink from the dangers that I meet.
- The enemy cannot get through the blood of Jesus that covers me.
- You cannot stand up to reality without God's will.
- When you are not walking in the will of God, then you are walking in the wrong place.
- The word of God activates the power of the Spirit within us.
- We need to learn to put our belief into action.
- Rich or poor, both need forgiveness.
- Be as willing to stand up as you are willing to bow down.
- Before I even ask, God knows my needs.
- I am a spiritualized individualization of good.
- It's time for our faith to shine as a beacon of His light unto the world.
- Hold good things to your heart and your spirit will flourish.
- Taking communion is an opportunity to fellowship at the Lord's table.
- May my soul magnify the Lord in every word and thought.

- My path at times can be winding and my turns can be wrong. Good Shepherd, just guide me to you where I belong.
- Lord, carry me safely to my destined place and bless my journey with your constant grace.
- The seed of God's love has been planted in your heart. It is up to you to water it, tend to it, nurture it, and pray for it to bloom into a beautiful flower.
- When we are a child of God, the act of kindness is never ending.
- God created a warm summer day to make the humblest daisy bloom so beautiful in every way.
- If you think that something is impossible, remember the empty tomb.
- Jesus is my everlasting light, for the word of God says with Him there is no darkness.
- Jesus, you have always cared about falling sparrows, lost dogs, and children who have gone astray. Thank you for caring about me.
- Wisdom and peace can lead to goodness, but foolishness can lead to the destruction of the soul.
- When we follow Jesus Christ, then we are a part of the Kingdom.
- Praising God is intimate. It's just between the two of you.
- When people reject the offer of salvation through Jesus Christ, then they are rejecting a precious gift from God.
- How changed our lives would be if we could only fly through the days on wings of surrendered praise and trust.

- Lord, always teach me to remember to never be too busy for someone when they are in need of prayer or a word of encouragement.
- He who cannot forgive others breaks the bridge over which he himself must pass into Heaven.
- Lord, I live in your transforming light. Let each day be filled with epiphanies and inspired clarity.
- Our faith will help us learn to look beyond the values of the world so that we might see the eternal values of God's Kingdom.
- I want to keep serving you, Lord, just like Paul did, for he became the leading missionary of early Christianity.
- We cannot have peace in our heart and soul until our enemies are under our feet.
- Waiting for something that you prayed for shows trust in God.
- The redeemed will reign with Christ. We can be optimistic about our future, not because of the circumstances that we see but because what God has promised us.
- Christ can heal our sickness whether they are spiritual or physical by natures.
- Christ is our wisdom, our righteousness, our sanctification, and our redemption.
- Speech is a unique gift from God if we put our words of belief into action.
- The Word of God says that we are to fear nothing but the Lord.
- Lord, teach me how to face the fears in my life through the power of the Holy Spirit and to trust in you always.

- When we are reckless and foolish then we can easily be defeated by Satan.
- When we have the love of God, it lives in our spirit, our souls, and the emotion of our hearts.
- Our trials and tribulations are just temporary when we are walking with Jesus by our side.
- When you speak to others, always speak with grace seasoned with the salt of the Word, and carry the love of God in your heart.
- By knowing God by our faith, it can make a big difference in our life.
- When we're hurting, the Lord wants to comfort us. When we are wounded, He wants to heal us. He wishes to nourish, feed, and strengthen his children. But, we as child of God must be willing to let that happen.
- You will know the peace of God when you know the God of peace.
- Through our patience, the scripture gives us comfort and hope.
- When Jesus is the source of your joy, no words can describe it.
- Don't ever be afraid to show your weakness to the Lord because by praying to Him, He can give you His strength.
- Step aside and let God go first, then everything else will fall into line.
- Jesus is the highest priest of all and there is no one higher.
- After Jesus shed his blood for us, then he rose victorious from the grave proclaiming victory over sin and death.

- Every experience that we go through with Jesus prepares us for our destiny.
- Time is a precious gift from God and must be used wisely.
- Every time I see daffodils or daisies growing on a hill, I see God's creation and whispering beauty as it stands still.
- Your faith will be destroyed when your focus is misdirected.
- Communion with God is a serious relationship. Great faith is often build during great trials.
- Lord, in humble sweet submission, here we meet and follow thee. Trusting is thy great salvation, which alone can set us free.
- To find salvation you must admit that you are lost.
- We must admit our weakness to experience God's strength. Always remember, God will take care of you and give you rainbows after the storm.
- It only takes a moment to be kind, but the result can last forever.
- Sin will keep you stumbling in the dark, but when you repent and ask God to forgive you. Then, you can walk in the light.
- There is only one road to heaven and Jesus leads the way.
- Nothing can compare to being with Jesus in heaven.
- God's love is a fountain from which all blessings flow.
- Jesus saw the needs of the children in Israel and he provided for them as he also provides for us.
- Hell is going to a place where Christ is not. Heaven is a place where Christ is.
- Many things can capture your eye, but let your faith in God capture your heart.

- God can give you daily blessings so you will be able to give Him the glory.
- Spirit of life, light, and love thy heavenly influence give. Quicken our souls and remove our guilt that we in Christ may live.
- Being fulfilled in Christ can be a wonderful blessing.
- Call upon Jesus, thy salvation, rest beneath almighty shade. In his secret habitation dwell and never be dismayed.
- We, as servants, will accomplish our missions only through the power of the Holy Spirit.
- There can always be a better and brighter day for God is just a prayer away.
- If your faith is weak and you've lost all hope, and your burdens are so heavy that you can't cope, remember God is there.
- When we stay closely committed to God, His spirit will enable us to do His will despite obstacles.
- Even our smallest acts of obedience and service can have widespread effects.
- God can still use someone despite the limitations and faith.
- Deep in our measurable minds of never failing skill, He instills in us His bright designs and works with his sovereign will.
- Beyond thy utmost wants, His love and power can bless. To praying souls, He always grants more than they can express.
- Come thou fount of every blessing, tune my heart to sing Thy grace. Streams of mercy never ceasing, call for songs of loudest praise.
- Faith can be stronger than fear.

- Our life can be like a garden, and our friendship like the flowers. They can bloom and grow in beauty with the sunshine and the showers.
- The world and weather changes, but one thing stays the same – Jesus!
- Sisters who are close at heart have a way of encouraging one another when they are in need.
- The word of God is full of knowledge that we need to learn and understand. The words become more familiar as we read them over and over again.
- When each one of us must harvest a field of faith, we must learn how to pluck out the weeds of doubt as it grows.
- Always release the power of God's word during challenging circumstances.
- It is better to be a follower who fails now and then than one who fails to follow God at all.
- God moves in mysterious ways His wonders to perform. He plants himself in the sea and He rides upon the storm.
- Satan never shall prevail; thou oh Christ shall never fail. We who fight with thee shall win, conquer over hell and sin.
- God loves us just the way we are, but he loves us too much to leave us that way.
- Prayer can make the darkest clouds withdraw. Climb the ladder that Jacob saw.
- Exercises in faith and love bring us blessing from above.
- When you have escaped from the wiles of the devil, remember you have not done it alone.

- Let Jesus fill you with the Holy Spirit. Give thanks that you have been led out of Egypt and you are beginning to walk to the Promised Land.
- Jesus made provision for all of us at Calvary.
- Make your hopes big hopes because God has designed greatness for you.
- When God directs us to begin a new walk of faith, there may be times when others do not walk with us.
- Always be willing to give God's love away with joy in your heart and no strings attached.
- Whenever we must make a decision, we must learn to look into His word.
- We should always try to follow the principles of praying and asking the Lord for guidance.
- Every time we think of God, it is because he first had us on his mind.
- Good friends stay close at heart, even when they are far apart.
- Those who know God's grace will show God's grace.
- Abide in me, Oh Lord, for I cannot bring forth good fruit all by myself.
- Lord, help me to be a cheerful friend who is always there to lend and bend.
- God, grant me life abundantly and guide me from above. Let your angels always hold me in the circle of your love.
- When we are willing to learn from our master, He will teach us how to live, love, and give.
- God's love is a gift to be treasured and shared, but don't wait to give it away.
- God, be with me today and help me to see your purpose in all of the trails along my life's journey.

- Every day we need to center our life in God. Always bring spiritual concentration into your prayer and your intercession.
- It's nice to know that God lives in us and that we can have the fellowship of His love.
- The valley of light will teach us the lesson of stillness. Let us learn to be still and let the inner light shine.
- Remember, just as fire purifies silver in the smelting process, our trials will refine our character.
- Remember Abraham and how he demonstrated his faith by obedience. He left his home to journey to an unknown land. Is your faith just as strong?
- Our God change the times and the seasons.
- Always pray in an honest and sincere manner.
- We must nourish our souls with the word of God daily so our spirit can survive; otherwise our soul would starve.
- Christ's blood not only covered our sins with redemptive love, but His stripes released a source of healing at every dimension of our need.
- Receive God as the Lord who heals you. His will is to make us well.
- God has a concern to restore every part of man; his personality, his health, and his relationship with Him.
- The Bible is history, promises, and simple instructions on how to live.
- The fruit of the spirit is good, productive, self-giving, nurturing, uplifting, and holy.
- There are different kinds of seeds that you can plant in good soil; seeds of love, faith, kindness, encouragement, forgiveness, hope, and peace.
- Our merciful God is the most compassionate and assuring spirit I have ever known.

- Jeremiah was one of the most successful people in all of history.
- Success must never be measured by popularity, fame, or fortune for these are temporary measures. God measures our success with the yardstick of obedience, faithfulness, and righteousness.
- Jeremiah was to be the mouthpiece of Jesus. He was to stand before the nation as a witness for truth and righteousness.
- Claim the victory in His holy name. You can do it because He wants you to.
- When you sow a seed of love, there will always be a good harvest.
- Ask humbly of your Father and you shall be blessed.
- Joy is the symphony of living. It is God's music concert in our hearts.
- We are not allowed to set terms with God. If we do, we lose.
- God is always doing little things for us; and sometimes they mean more than the bigger things.
- We all sin and we all fall short of God's glorious standards, but one thing I do know - He forgives.
- God's presence should motivate each one of us to live a life that is pleasing to Him.
- When Jesus completely forgives you, He wants you to follow His example by forgiving others.
- When we accept Jesus Christ as our Savior we can live with peace in our hearts.
- Today is enough to bear. When tomorrow comes, His grace shall far exceed its cares.
- We should view our difficulties not as obstacles to our faith, but as opportunities for spiritual growth.
- Defend and stand up for Jesus. He does it for you.

- God can use anything you must offer so His plans can be known.
- We can be fed daily by reading our Bible.
- If you follow Jesus Christ and listen for His voice, your life will overflow with His blessings and your days will be filled with joy.
- You are very special to Jesus and the angels rejoiced the day you were born.
- When we are living by pride we are not living a lifestyle that is surrendered to the Lord.
- When we begin to think we can handle things by ourselves, then we stop relying on God and stop seeking Him in prayer.
- Resist all wicked spirits and pride. Apply His name and word daily.
- Lord, I have gained wisdom and understanding by the lessons you have taught me.
- We must learn to do everything for the glory of God, not for ourselves.
- Don't forget to glorify our Almighty God, for He is good all the time.
- If you do not forgive someone then you are still living in sin yourself. Forgive that person so your Heavenly Father can forgive you. The Bible says pray for your enemy and forgive.
- The Lord never fails to save a soul, but a fool will dwell in sin.
- When we are in prayer with God, we need to stay focused solely on Him. We need to be still and listen for His voice.
- When we open our hearts and live by His faith and love, we can find out just what God is capable of.

- God is looking for more people to be like Abraham and to be committed to Him and to refuse doubt.
- God may show you to share His covenant with those who do not know Jesus Christ as their Savior.
- Jesus - what a wonderful companion.
- The seagulls gang around me like a group of Christian friends; and as I begin to smile among them, my sorrow spirit ends.
- It takes no special talent, it makes no difference who you are, to light just one little candle that outshines the brightest star.
- I look for a quiet place to seek His presence and by His grace I find it.
- Faith believes and focuses on proclaiming God's Word without reservation.
- By sharing Jesus with others, it will give us a deeper insight into our inheritance with Christ.
- Let Jesus and His Word be the foundation and sustainer of your thinking.
- As followers of God, we need to give our love to Jesus first place in our lives and to commit ourselves both emotionally and intellectually.
- Measure your conduct and attitude regularly according to God's Word.
- Sometimes we need to change our hearts as well as our behavior.
- Always understand that it is the presence of Jesus that produces glory.
- Friendship is caring for one another and being there when they are in need.

- Do not throw away your confidence in Him, for He will not fail you. Continue to persevere in doing His will and you will receive what He has promised you. It will be worth the wait.
- As you trust and rely on Jesus completely; His power can be at work in you. Then He can give you far above what you ask.
- You are His child and He takes great delight in you. Do not recall your past mistakes for you have asked for His forgiveness and you know He has forgiven you. You can stand pure and holy in His presence.
- He chose you and called you to come to Him. When you came and accepted Jesus Christ as your Savior, He declared you not guilty. He washed you clean with His blood and filled you with His goodness.
- Do not ever doubt His love for you, for He proved how much He loves you by sending His Son to take the punishment for your sins. It was not because of your love for Him that He did this, but because of His great love for you.
- When you call upon Him and ask Him for His strength, He can hear your voice and your request.
- Have you ever stopped to think that the Lord wants the best for you? He is your Heavenly Father and it pleases Him greatly to see you prosper in every area of your life.
- Abraham, David, Daniel, King Jehoshaphat, Moses, and Paul chose to worship Him in the midst of their trials and He brought them through in victory. So, offer up to Him a sacrifice of praise my child. He will do the same for you.
- God can give us a song to sing for every different circumstance in our life.

- God's Word will prosper if it is in you.
- You can't play hide and seek from God. You either hide from Him like Adam or you seek Him like David.
- Stay focused on your visions and your dreams that God has given to you. For they are your ultimate achievements.
- We should constantly devote our will to God.
- Temptations seldom come through the front door of life, they usually slip through an open window or slide down the chimney.
- We must overcome all that tears people apart and pray on all that brings people together.
- The love of God that you give to others is the best medicine in every situation.
- Are you trying to find someone to understand you? The Lord understands.
- If you are living in the past, you cannot reach your new destiny that God has for you.
- Troubles will not make me angry or cause me to live in distress, because I know that the Lord keeps me in His peacefulness.
- Our Christian life with Jesus Christ involves hard work. We must give up everything that will endanger our walk and relationship with Him.
- The only way to escape from the devil is to flee into the arms of Jesus.
- We cannot build a ladder high enough to reach God. He reaches down to us.
- To trust in God is to have immeasurable peace.
- Once you have prayed for something, start thanking Him.

- Ask God to renew His powerful presence in your life and He will.
- When you are disobedient to God, He will not grant you a spiritual victory.
- Our daily prayers should always include protection and physical, mental, emotional and spiritual guidance. We should always pray for peace, encouragement, and strength through our Lord Jesus Christ.
- Friendship and love are golden threads that tie the heart from hate.
- When we have nothing left but Christ; we find out that He is enough.
- If you have wisdom to teach, share it. If you have the heart to love, show it.
- I sought to hear the voice of God, so I climbed to the top of the steeple. But God declared go down again and dwell among the people.
- We can't see the Holy Spirit, but we can feel His presence. Did you ever feel the breeze from the wind? You know it's there but you can't see it.
- Always give the Lord the best that you have. Serve Him from clean motives. To offer the Lord less than our best is unworthy of His Holy Name.
- God wants His people to be fully devoted to Him. We are to seek God's face continually, expressing our wholehearted devotion to Him. We need to understand that the Lord's calling in our life is based on His power and not on our natural abilities.
- If we feed God's flock willingly, we will receive an eternal crown of glory when the Chief Shepherd appears.

- The richest people in the world are those who are content with what they have no matter how little it may be.
- God is mightier than anything. He is more powerful than any person I know.
- He, like us, grew tired, hungry, and sad; it is in His Word to see. But He knew that God would not fail to help Him, help you, and help me.
- Doing what God desires us to do is the greatest possible life investment.
- When you are called to be a prophet like Isaiah, you are to respond by grace, love, and faith.
- Just when I think I have given up and things are going wrong; You bring gladness into my heart and I'm never troubled long.
- God will answer your prayers in time and your blessings can multiply by the millions.
- When the ten thousand years are finished, He will descend to the earth made new. Oh, how happy we will be then and what glorious scenes we will view. Has the journey seemed too long to you? Come rest awhile by the river. Partake of the tree of life and travel with Jesus forever.
- The wicked run when no one is chasing them, but an honest person is as brave as the lion.
- Let God's presence in your life be known and felt.
- If we accept defeat from the enemy, we will never see the victory with Jesus.
- The Cross isn't medicine, but it is a cure. Go to the Cross today and don't delay. Repent and ask forgiveness, then you can begin a new life with Jesus.
- The meaning of the Cross just isn't the wood it's made of; it's the sacrifice that Jesus made for all of us.

- We will never know the complete cost of Jesus sacrificing His life for our sins on the Cross at Calvary; but we can begin to understand the value of His gift to us.
- Love is a spiritual force; you sow it and you will see it.
- We need to be more like David and focus on the prize and not the problem.
- Sometimes what we listen to can weaken our faith, so be careful.
- Upon the Cross of Calvary, Jesus suffered for you and me. They scourged, they mocked, and they spit in His face. It was for us that He took our place. For us the spear was thrust in His side. For us He bled and died. For us He left heaven's glory. For us this is the greatest story.
- Jesus, you have taught me how to follow, and the power to lead, and to achieve things I thought I couldn't do.
- Take time to do some charity today, for you may find a friend who has lost their way. Never be selfish, take time to give, so others around you can begin to live.
- Show them the power of prayer that God has given to you, and your loving kindness will always shine through.
- 'Tis the good news of salvation, the Savior's great desire to bless, we reach out and claim it by faith, this pure robe of His righteousness. This blessing does not come by works, lest we should be inclined to boast. Yet the ones that serve the Master are the ones that love Him most.
- God calls us by our name and we learn to obey. He exalts His laws and His teachings.

- Before you go to sleep tonight, don't forget to pray. Thank the Lord for all He's done and His blessings for today.
- Faith is doing what you believe in, and our faith works by love, not by strife.
- Friendship is a chain from God shaped in God's all perfect mold. Each link is a smile or laughter, for it is treasured more than gold. No matter how far or heavy the load, sweet is the journey on friendship road.
- Jesus has a way of loving and comforting us when we need it the most. He is your light when it is dark and your anchor at all times.
- A mother never forgets where her children are, neither does Christ.
- Our sincere prayers to God are never wasted. Every day we must pray for those who are sick and need the healing from God. Most of those we pray for do recover.
- Slow me down Lord, so I can listen to my heart and see with my eyes the source of my life which is you.
- A false witness tells lies, but a truthful witness can give an honest testimony. If we forsake Jesus, we are not living Godly.
- I feel a flutter in my heart as I see the rising sun. The eastern sky is tinted bright as the new day has begun. The morning glories come to life in the stillness of the morn. A peacefulness prevails as another day is born.
- Without God, we are like the wick of a candle that has never met fire, even though we exist, we cannot shine.
- When you walk away from Jesus you have just closed a door.
- God dwells wherever man lets Him in.

- When you are serving God, you need a heart filled with grace and a soul generated by love.
- If the devil can defeat your mind, then he can defeat your heart.
- When you have two hands and a kind heart to help others, that is love.
- The Lord is our Shepherd and we are His sheep, do not break the flock.
- Faith can give you peace from the past, grace for the present, and hope for the future.
- God's love is the fountain from which all our blessings flow.
- It takes two to quarrel, but only one to apologize.
- Jesus is eternally refreshing water. Let Him quench your spiritual thirst.
- To build a godly life, let God be the architect and His Word be the blueprint.
- To walk in peace, keep in step with Jesus.
- To find salvation you must admit to God that you are lost.
- Jesus is the true peacemaker in your life.
- God is more concerned with the quality of our prayers than the quantity.
- The victory of our battles is ours if we do not take it on by ourselves.
- God can give you daily blessings so you can give Him glory.
- You will always be a target for the enemy when you are a Christian. Always keep praying for protection.
- Let your worry drain out and let your peace flow in.
- You can have victory over your battles when you remember who is in charge.
- Soft words are pillows for hurt.

- Hold the good things in your heart and your spirit will flourish.
- I look at the chapel upon the hill as it stands so quiet and still. But as I look at the steeple that is so tall, the Cross stands out most of all.
- Looking out at the evening sky at night is drawing near, I know Jesus is close to me and I have nothing to fear.
- As we walk down a long country road, we must give all our problems to Jesus and let Him carry the load.
- Our lives are like ships in the night. He gives us strength to stay on course and to challenge all things with spiritual force.
- Do not get disheartened and do not let the skies turn gray, for the Lord will shine His light upon you and make it a sun shiny day.
- Our Heavenly Father is our Daddy; and we will never get to old for our Daddy's love.
- We as Christians are not to adapt to the world's way of thinking or it's standards of behavior.
- Lord, make me an honest and faithful servant so I can always serve you first and then the people.
- Lord, when I feel small and insignificant, remind me that in your eyes I am special.
- Lord, no matter what I do, you never give up on me.
- Lord, when opportunities come knocking at my door, teach me to walk out by my faith so I can receive them.
- Sweetly the light is shining for thee. Remember the Light of the World is Jesus.
- We need time to pray because it is a vital link with God.
- Mantle - The mantle is the anointing of God.

- Never complain about your hardships to others, for God designed them so you can be trained for maturity.
- God is the source of all blessings.
- God is able to supply your every need, even when you have no idea how.
- We must never allow anything to become more important to us than our pursuit of God.
- We must understand that the glory of God is revealed to those who believe.
- One of the key words in John's gospel is believe.
- You can have success in your life when you let Jesus live in your heart.
- It's useless to look elsewhere for something God alone can give.
- The Bible's purpose is to light our way, not to cover our tracks.
- Jesus lifted me up instead of letting me down.
- Jesus changed my life. No one else could do it.
- People can come against us and they can inflict pain, suffering, or even death, but the good news is no one can rob us of our souls.
- Prayer can quiet our thoughts and emotions and it can prepare us to listen.
- Nothing deep within our mind and heart can be hidden from God.
- When you are not walking in the will of God, you are in the wrong place.
- Where we find the shelter that God has for us, the storms in our life will not seem so fierce.
- Always worship God with a purified heart.
- Obeying Jesus is the primary evidence that we love Him.

- We as believers are to be unified in our devotion to the Gospel of Christ. Acknowledging where we have fallen short and repent.
- Wherever we go, whatever we do, we are never alone.
- Our precious Savior is always and will always be our Refuge.
- When we find out that praise is centered by God, we are the ones who are changed by it.
- To do God's will, obey His Word.
- God always sees below the surface.
- If you keep your eyes upon the Lord and you should happen to stumble, He will lift you up.
- Give God your heart and the rest will follow.
- Build a life of truth and it will not collapse.
- The Word of God is a book to read. It isn't a puzzle to be solved.
- Prayer is a conversation with the King of Kings. The life that Christ can give can last forever.
- Lord, may our desire for you grow into our heart and soul with delight.
- Get out of fear and into faith.
- We must balance our prayers. Let your request be known to God. There are different elements of prayer: supplication, confession, thanksgiving and adoration.
- Learn to pray with faith and believe and you can receive.
- For He is our Provider, Redeemer, Light, and Salvation.
- When we pray sincerely great things begin to happen in our lives.
- Don't ever forget who created you. Give Him praise every day.

- We can get deceived easily if we follow our emotions instead of Jesus.
- The stormy clouds are not in view when you know Jesus is watching over you.
- God does not shine the light in your heart to hide it. He shines the light in your heart to show it.
- Give and keep giving, love and keep loving.
- Start your day the right way. Have a little prayer with Jesus.
- For each day brings life anew, for He has given it to you.
- God's promise is better than anyone's promise.
- The Lord will grant me strength and His love will sustain me.
- When we harvest a godly harvest, we will always see fruit unto life eternally.
- You never walk alone; for Jesus is always with you.
- When we fellowship with the Lord, it's always a wonderful reunion.
- Never pass up an opportunity of seeing anything beautiful, for beauty is God's handwriting. Always welcome it with peace, love, and joy. Don't ever forget to thank God, for it is a blessing.
- Biblical wisdom means purity, godliness, and virtue.
- I am a woman like you are. I am a mother like you are. Yet because we live separate lives, through Jesus Christ we can still come in agreement and love one another.
- Nature meets many of man's needs. Among other things he finds beauty for his soul, healing for his body, knowledge for his inquiring mind, communication with his Creator, and peace for his troubled heart.

- In heights of glory we will stand living by God's Word and walking hand in hand.
- Go out and help a brother or sister today, but be aware of the traps the enemy sets for you.
- God says the Holy Spirit is my price, so another generous soul can be enriched.
- When you are saved by the grace of God, He will show you His true relevance.
- The more we pray, read, and hear about Jesus, the more we can believe in Him and the stronger our faith can become.
- When your world begins to shake, run to the Rock.
- When we repent for our sins, He saves. When we ask for forgiveness, He forgives. When we live our life for Christ, we are His temple, His house, and His home. He is Master and Builder of our life, for He is our Lord God Almighty.
- When we care about God's children, we are honoring God and helping to build His kingdom.
- Walking through another valley is a true test of our faith. As we are walking through another valley we will discover that our faith is our life support equipment. It is also a test of our spiritual and emotional well being.
- We must maintain a spiritual balance when a problem comes. Don't ever allow any problem, person or situation to get into your spirit or it will get ahold and take control of your emotions and your heart.
- Snowflakes and fingerprints you can always find, each one of them are different and one of a kind. And just like a snowflake, this is so true, nothing or no one is created exactly like you.

- Our spiritual vision is our capacity to see clearly what God wants us to do and to see the world from His point of view, not ours.
- There is only one Divine Healer and His name is Jesus.
- By reviving hope and faith, they show the soul it's living powers, and how beneath the winter's snow, lie germs of summer flowers.
- The cleansing of our sins cannot work from the outside. It has to work from the inside out.
- In times of distress, keep looking to God for the assurance you need to face life with courage.
- The sunshine lives in my heart today, for Jesus has forgiven me and washed all my sins away.
- Jesus Christ chose us out of the world, not by chance, but by choice.
- God resists the proud but gives grace to the humble. We have a choice: either be proud like the devil or humble like Christ.
- His strength and His power keep flowing deep into my heart.
- The Lord's hands will keep us safe from our enemies and we will cling to Him like a leaf on a tree.
- A flower cannot blossom without a seed first being planted.
- Oh Lord, give me the spirit of wisdom and revelation so I can get to know You better.
- The Ten Commandments provide us with the best guidelines for an effective fulfilling life.
- God is never too early or too late. He is always on time.

- Please Lord, always fill my heart and soul with knowledge and understanding so I can always walk in a manner that is worthy of you.
- If we do not find time for prayer, many of the good things that should happen in our lives will not happen.
- An echo of your name is found in every breath and every sound. To whom all praise is to be given, to our Eternal God who is in heaven.
- When we say that we are fully committed to God, we must think seriously about what is involved.
- Fervent believing prayer will unlock doors. It will solve problems, bring healing, and will help you win victories over Satan.
- As Christians, sometimes we need to come together and pray, for God will intervene on our behalf. God rules overall and will triumph over evil.
- Sometimes the Lord will have you climb a tall mountain so you can praise Him in a higher place.
- The taste of honey is sweet, but the Lord is sweeter.
- Throw a life preserver to a friend. Let them know you have a good heart and a helping hand.
- One of nature's lessons is that death is a part of life. Seeds die in the ground but they germinate new plants. Leaves die on the trees but new leaves return in the spring. Man dies. but the good news is that we can have eternal life with Jesus.
- Our trials of testing can make our faith stronger.
- The presence of the risen Christ prepares us to witness by the power of the Holy Spirit.
- Refuse to worry about your circumstances, just keep trusting the Lord.
- A real friend makes a difference in your life without choosing your path for you.

- When the Lord lets us hear a robin sing, then we know it isn't long until spring.
- Even our smallest acts of obedience and service can have widespread effects.
- Get out of fear and into faith.
- The wise wait on Jesus, but the foolish think Jesus should wait on them.
- Through the cross we are made acceptable to Jesus Christ.
- Not even our tiniest teardrops go by without being noticed by our Heavenly Father.
- When I go to my hidden place of prayer, it is my quiet cathedral and I will find my Jesus there.
- You will always be a target for the enemy when you are a Christian, so keep praying for protection.
- We are children of God and He wants us to grow into spiritual adulthood, but it requires the hand of time.
- Doubt will push you right into a valley.
- To grow spiritually we need to face our failures. Then we can focus on Jesus Christ in the future.
- Lord, come tonight and kiss my eyes, then carry my dreams to heaven's skies.
- Dear Father, I pray that you will be with me every day so that I can become the kind of Christian whose words and actions reflect on your Son Jesus.
- Give your all to the Lord and trust Him with every beat of your heart.
- Our actions are affected by the things we dwell on.
- Remember Jesus was a master of illustrations. He used natural occurrences in life to show timeless principles.
- When we are taking our steps in the same direction with Jesus, then we know they are the right steps.

- Our Father, help us to make your name, your kingdom, and your will the top priorities in our lives.
- Hear me O Lord, in time of my prayer. I cry with my voice and I make my supplication. Lord, you are my Refuge, my King, my Master, and my loving Father. You have brought my soul out of prison and You have delivered me from my sins. For You have dealt with me bountifully. You have freed me from evil and wickedness. You have given me happiness and new life. Lord, You have blessed me and given me peace. I will keep Thy commandments for ever and ever. Amen.
- The tree of life is transplanted in the paradise of our Lord. The leaves hang low over the wall that we may partake and be restored. We should partake of it daily to be spiritually strong as steel. Believe His precious promises for they are the ones that heal.
- How precious is His assurance when we know that He is present?
- The sweetest song can come from a broken heart.
- Never be hopeless or in doubt, with Jesus as our Savior all things will work out.
- Jesus is like a silversmith who watches a furnace of fire. To see reflected in silver, His own image, He doth desire. Fiery trials make golden Christians. He beholds who doth Him behold. And if you stand the fiery trials, you will come forth as purest gold.
- Remember Satan is not after the unsaved. He is after those who are saved.
- When the tears are flowing like a river and they are running down your face, remember the love of Jesus and His amazing grace.

- Practice obedience to God's Word and apply it every day of your life. Read it. Believe it. Live it.
- There is power in the seed that you plant if it is Godly.
- When we face painful things today, we can use them for stepping stones for tomorrow.
- My youth is gone but now I am advancing into my golden years with God.
- When our children are grown, then we, as parents, have to let go and let God.
- Our God is full of abundance and blessings. We learn to live in His goodness and Grace.
- Life can be difficult and uncertain, so keep your faith in Jesus at all times.
- Some say there will be Miracles that happen today. When the sky is clear and blue, listen and watch my friends, because one of the Miracles may just be for you.
- God has a way of giving us true and loyal friends that will walk with us through life's journey to the very end.
- Jesus can give you some vacation in peace, for He can provide it all.
- When Autumn comes, we get to see a beautiful Harvest Time display of red, yellow, orange and gold. It is His wonders to behold.
- Watching a child grow is like watching a flower blossom. It's a miracle and it's more than you could ever hope for.
- We need to reach out with loving and caring hands, and then God will show us the joy of human kindness.
- When we do Godly things for others, we never give it a second thought. We just do it.

- God does not create our suffering and pain, but he can offer us Grace and strength to endure.

THE END

IT'S ONLY THE BEGINNING
WITH JESUS

Made in the USA
Columbia, SC
04 November 2023